SEEFELD

TRAVEL GUIDE
2023

Seefeld: The Ideal Christmas Getaway: A
Complete Guide to the Town's Festivities,
Shopping, and More. What to See, Do, and Eat

NICOLAS MENDEZ

1

Table Of Contents

INTRODUCTION

GETTING STARTED: Your Gateway to Seefeld's Winter Marvels

DISCOVERING SEEFELD: Unveiling the Charms of an Alpine Jewel

CHRISTMAS FESTIVITIES OVERVIEW

WINTER ACTIVITIES: Embracing Alpine Thrills in Seefeld

DINING AND CULINARY DELIGHTS

SHOPPING GUIDE: Unveiling Seefeld's Winter Treasures

ENTERTAINMENT AND NIGHTLIFE: Revelry Amidst Alpine Splendor

FAMILY-FRIENDLY ACTIVITIES: Winter Adventures for All Ages in Seefeld

PRACTICAL TIPS FOR A MERRY VISIT TO SEEFELD'S WINTER WONDERLAND

DAY TRIPS AND EXCURSIONS: Exploring Beyond Seefeld's Winter Magic

LOCAL INSIGHTS: Seefeld Unveiled through Interviews and Christmas Stories

SEEFELD ON A BUDGET: Unveiling Affordable Delights in the Alpine Haven

A MAGICAL CHRISTMAS IN SEEFELD: Sample Itinerary to Embrace the Festive Spirit

CONCLUSION: A Winter Wonderland Farewell from Seefeld

BONUS: COOKING UP SEEFELD CHRISTMAS DELIGHTS: Festive Recipes from the Alpine Wonderland

INTRODUCTION

Explore the quaint Alpine town of Seefeld with our all-inclusive travel guide for 2023 and set out on a joyous adventure. Seefeld, tucked away among snow-capped peaks, becomes a Christmas wonderland during the holiday season, providing a special fusion of winter magic and tradition.

Discover a warm welcome to this enchanted location in our introduction, where we lay the groundwork for your vacation experiences. Learn about the goals of the guide so that you may easily traverse Seefeld's holiday offerings.

This introduction invites you to appreciate the excitement and beauty that distinguish Seefeld throughout the holiday season, from the sparkling lights adorning the streets to the aroma of mulled wine floating through the air.

Welcome to Seefeld: Embracing Alpine Elegance

i) **Welcome to Seefeld**

Seefeld, tucked away in the Austrian Alps, welcomes you to a wintry paradise that goes beyond typical vacation spots. A symphony of snow-covered pine trees and cool mountain air welcomes you as you enter this picture-perfect Alpine village, laying the groundwork for an amazing Christmas experience.

Seefeld's timeless appeal is characterized by its peaceful white scenery painted by majestic peaks, cobblestone streets, and quaint chalets. A pleasant greeting from a local willing to share the wonder of their winter paradise reflects the town's warm hospitality. Seefeld's warm embrace ensures a vacation unlike any other, whether you're looking for a family outing or a romantic getaway.

ii) **About this Guide**

Your key to discovering the mysteries of Seinfeld's captivating Christmas events is our guide. This guide, which has been painstakingly and passionately edited, is intended for both novice and experienced travelers. Its pages contain a multitude of information that has been painstakingly compiled to make sure your trip to Seefeld is smooth and enjoyable.

Explore in-depth information on the town's customs, history, and distinctive blend of traditions that contribute to its very magical Christmas celebrations. This book intends to be your go-to resource, giving you the confidence to navigate Seefeld and make the most of every moment, from useful advice to exciting experiences.

iii) **Getting Around Seefeld at Christmas**

During the Christmas season, Seefeld becomes a jovial spectacle, and making your way through its offerings demands consideration. Our guide gives you the skills you need to handle the town's winter environment, so your exploration and leisure time go hand in hand.

Explore the nuances of Seefeld's Christmas markets, where the sounds of carolers blend with the aroma of roasted chestnuts. Find the ideal paths for a charming winter stroll through the town center, which is decked out with festive storefronts and sparkling lights.

Whether you want to enjoy the calm of a fireside conversation in a classic Austrian café or the excitement of winter sports, our guide offers a blueprint for planning the perfect Seefeld Christmas.

Take in the lively atmosphere of the town square as you stroll about Seefeld over the holidays. Here, the classic Christmas tree takes center stage. It is embellished with traditional decorations and brilliant lights, making it an enticing focal point for holiday get-togethers.

Discover the quaint Christmas market stalls, where regional craftspeople display their handmade goods and the aroma of cloves and cinnamon fills the air. Our guide helps you discover the true essence of Seefeld's holiday charm, making sure you don't pass over the well-known sites and lesser-known attractions that turn the town into a winter wonderland.

Our expert suggests visiting Seefeld's historic churches for a more reflective experience since they host Christmas Eve services that bring centuries-old customs to life. As locals and visitors alike gather in song and contemplation, fostering a sense of oneness amid the bitter cold of winter, you can feel the warmth of community. Discovering Seefeld in the Christmas season involves more than just exploring the area physically; it also involves embracing the spirit of the occasion, and our guide offers the knowledge you need to take advantage of all the festivities to offer.

To put it briefly, our book serves as your ticket to an unforgettable Christmas in Seefeld, providing a warm welcome to the town's Alpine elegance, in-depth analyses of its distinct charm, and a road map for discovering all the joyous festivities that lie ahead. Our guide will make sure that every moment of your journey is full of happiness, exploration, and the timeless magic of a white Christmas in the Austrian Alps. Seefeld beckons.

GETTING STARTED: Your Gateway to Seefeld's Winter Marvels

Travel Essentials

To guarantee a smooth and pleasurable trip, it is important to carefully evaluate the necessary travel items before setting out on a tour to Seefeld. Packing proper winter clothing, such as thermal accessories, waterproof boots, and insulated layers, should come first.

Because of the cool Alpine weather, it's important to come prepared so you can enjoy the breathtaking scenery without discomfort. Remember to include necessities like travel adapters and make sure your electronics are fully charged so you can record the breathtaking moments Seefeld has to offer.

Having some euros on hand and being aware of the local currency is equally important. Even though credit cards are generally accepted, having cash on hand is useful, particularly in marketplaces and smaller businesses. It's a good idea to get winter activity-specific travel insurance so you may enjoy peace of mind while participating in Seefeld's winter sports and festive events.

Accommodation Options

Seefeld has a variety of lodging choices, each of which enhances a memorable stay amidst the snow-capped peaks. Select from luxurious hotels with lavish amenities or classic Alpine chalets that give a genuine mountain experience. Cozy bed & breakfasts in the town provide a more personal touch, while vacation rentals offer flexibility for larger groups or extended visits.

If you want to experience Seefeld's Christmas charm, you might want to book accommodations close to the town center. Because of its close vicinity, Seefeld's holiday markets, events, and glittering lights are all easily accessible. Seek lodgings with expansive views of the neighboring mountains so you can enjoy a breathtaking Alpine landscape every morning when you wake up.

Transportation Guide

A well-thought-out transportation guide makes navigating Seefeld's winter paradise simple. The closest major airport, Innsbruck Airport, is about 20 kilometers distant if you're arriving by plane. You can go to Seefeld immediately from there via a variety of transportation choices, such as shuttle services and taxis. Another reasonable choice is Munich Airport, as train services may get you from Munich to Seefeld in a matter of hours.

Once at Seefeld, you can explore its quaint streets and lively markets on foot because the town is small and walkable. Local buses and taxis offer convenient transportation for larger distances and if you're carrying equipment for winter activities. Seefeld's public transportation system is quite efficient, which makes it simple to get to neighboring destinations and enjoy winter activities.

Renting a car gives you flexibility and the chance to go on beautiful drives through the Alpine scenery if you intend to explore the area. Remember that driving in the winter may necessitate the use of snow chains and that you should always check the road conditions and weather reports before embarking on a journey.

A system of well-kept paths connects Seefeld to other areas for winter sports lovers. Popular winter sports include skiing, snowboarding, and snowshoeing, and the town offers quick access to a variety of routes fit for hikers of all ability levels. If you didn't bring your equipment, think about renting it from nearby stores or resorts.

To sum up, beginning your Seefeld journey requires careful planning and consideration of lodging, transportation, and other necessary travel items. Make sure you are prepared for the winter weather, choose a lodging that meets your needs, and know how to get around.

These steps lay the groundwork for an enjoyable and stress-free tour of Seefeld's winter wonders. Seefeld is waiting to be discovered, with its charming winter scenery and festive offerings. With our all-inclusive guide, your trip will be smooth and enjoyable.

DISCOVERING SEEFEID: Unveiling the Charms of an Alpine Jewel

Historic Landmarks

Seefeld's history is richly woven together by a plethora of historic landmarks, many of which date back to the Middle Ages. The famous Seekirchl, also known as Seekirche, is a church whose history is as fascinating as its stunning design. According to legend, the person who built it was a local who, on the adjacent lake, miraculously survived a storm. A must-see is the church, with its distinctive green onion dome shining brightly against the wintry surroundings.

Discover the magnificence of the town's principal parish church, Pfarrkirche St. Oswald. Its elaborate interior and Gothic architecture, which date to the fifteenth century, highlight centuries' worth of religious and cultural value. The church's quiet environs offer a tranquil haven, and guests are frequently invited to watch classical music given inside its revered walls.

Discover the past in the Wildsee, a picturesque lake encircled by dense trees. Although it's a beautiful place to visit now, it was formerly a bog from which people collected peat to make fuel. A walking track circles the lake, showcasing the ruins of this old peat-cutting operation and providing amazing views of the mountains all around.

Regional Traditions and Cultures

Discover the colorful local culture of Seefeld and immerse yourself in its beloved customs to truly experience the city's heart. The traditional garb worn on festive occasions is a testament to the town's pride in maintaining its Tyrolean heritage. Observe the people dressed in dirndls and lederhosen, who liven up the wintry scenery with their vibrant attire.

Savor the food of Tyrolea, a fundamental aspect of Seefeld culture, by not passing up this opportunity. Savor filling fare like käsespätzle (**cheese noodles**) and Tiroler gröstl (**pan-fried potatoes with meat**), which are served in quaint hütten (**mountain taverns**). In addition to serving up wonderful food, these rustic eateries offer a window into the kind hospitality that characterizes Tyrolean culture.

Take part in the customary celebrations to feel the happiness of a Tyrolean Christmas. The town's Christmas markets are vibrant centers of holiday cheer as well as places to purchase handcrafted goods and regional specialties. Attend local events featuring traditional music and dance, where the celebratory ambiance is created by the echoing folk tunes and the rhythmic movements of the dancers.

Take part in the long-standing tradition of the Krampuslauf, a parade that features the legendary Alpine monster Krampus. Folklore-based custom: during the Christmas season, residents dress up as Krampus and prowl the streets in extravagant costumes and scary masks. It gives the joyful mood a thrilling and slightly unsettling touch.

Hidden Gems

Seefeld's charm goes beyond its well-known sights; astute tourists are bound to find hidden treasures that lie in wait. Nestled in the Olympiaregion Seefeld, the charming village of Mösern provides a peaceful haven. Admire the stunning views of the surrounding mountains and the Inn Valley as you meander through the town's winding lanes adorned with quaint homes.

Discover the natural wonder known as Leutascher Geisterklamm, or Leutasch Ghost Gorge, which is only a short drive from Seefeld. This valley transports you into the unspoiled splendor of the Tyrolean Alps with its wooden paths and bridges. For those who love the outdoors, this hidden gem is a haven of lush foliage, towering cliffs, and murmuring rivers that create a lovely atmosphere.

Visit the Lautersee, a gorgeous mountain lake encircled by thick trees, for a peaceful getaway. A serene path encircles the lake, providing a serene environment for reflection. The lake's surface is reflected from the surrounding peaks, creating a captivating scene that is perfect for a leisurely stroll or some alone time.

The Rosshütte, a year-round adventure hub as well as a popular skiing destination, is located in the center of Seefeld. It's a dream come true for skiers and snowboarders in the winter and a mountain biker and hiker's paradise in the summer. Visitors of all ages can enjoy the varied activities and breathtaking views from the panoramic cable car ride to the summit.

You'll learn that Seefeld's real charm is a combination of its active local culture, well-preserved history, and the finding of hidden treasures as you explore these hidden gems. Together, these components produce an immersive experience that defies description and beckons you to immerse yourself in Seefeld's engrossing tale.

CHRISTMAS FESTIVITIES OVERVIEW

The Magic of Seefeld's Christmas

Seefeld is enveloped in a layer of snow and, come Christmastime, seems to have taken on the qualities of a fantasy land, captivating both tourists and residents. The evergreen aroma of the fresh Alpine air permeates the town, and the glittering lights add to the ethereal atmosphere. Seefeld's Christmas magic is found in its ability to combine tradition with winter's charm, creating a heartwarming celebration amidst the picturesque scenery.

The town's central square, with its imposing Christmas tree serving as a symbol of holiday cheer, is the hub of all this beauty. The tree becomes the center of attention for joyous parties when it is decked out with sparkling lights and classic decorations. Both locals and tourists congregate, enjoying the cheer of the season while sipping mulled wine.

The sound of timeless classics being played by carolers is irresistible and cannot be stopped. The soft crunch of snow beneath your feet paired with the melodic vocals provide a soundtrack that elevates the entire Christmas experience. Seefeld comes alive during this season, with a strong sense of community and a prevalent spirit of giving and togetherness.

Traditional Christmas Markets

The traditional Seefeld Christmas markets are a highlight of the holiday season. The town is transformed by the markets into a vibrant display of stalls with festive décor and the enticing smell of Christmas fare. Located in the heart of the town, the main market is a kaleidoscope of hues and sounds, with a lovely selection of handcrafted goods, regional specialties, and festive décor.

Stalls offering handcrafted candles, ornaments with exquisite designs, and traditional Tyrolean crafts await you as you stroll about. These items would make ideal Christmas presents or mementos. Local craftspeople display their abilities, fostering a market environment that highlights the genuineness of Tyrolean craftsmanship.

Treat your palate to delectable food in the Christmas markets. A wide variety of seasonal delights are available at the market stalls, ranging from delicious pastries to sizzling sausages. Enjoy a warm cup of mulled wine, or glühwein, and indulge in some local specialties to fully experience the flavors of Tyrolean cuisine.

The Seefeld Christmas markets frequently have a vintage carousel and other traditional fairground items for a nostalgic touch. These upgrades provide an immersive experience that takes guests to a bygone age and evokes a sense of timeless seasonal charm.

Festive Event and Celebrations

Seefeld's holiday schedule is jam-packed with activities and festivities that enhance the Christmas season. The annual Advent Concert at the **Pfarrkirche St. Oswald** is one of the highlights. The church's Gothic style makes for a stunning setting for local musicians' and choirs' performances. The centuries-old walls are filled with resonant tones of classical and celebratory music, creating an ethereal and enchanting ambiance that defies time.

Take in the splendor of the **Christmas Eve Torchlight Parade,** a spectacle that casts a warm glow of flickering torches over the wintry countryside. Residents parade through the town dressed for the holidays, casting a luminous symphony against the wintry night. This captivating custom represents the victory of light over darkness, a concept that is closely linked to the spirit of Christmas.

The Children's Christmas Festival is a kid-friendly event that is sure to win over hearts. The festival consists of a mix of happy activities, storytelling sessions, and interactive games, with Santa Claus making a special appearance. It is evidence of Seefeld's dedication to provide a healthy Christmas experience for guests of all ages.

On New Year's Eve, as the clock approaches midnight, Seefeld bursts into a brilliant display of fireworks that create a rainbow-colored night sky. Both locals and tourists congregate in the town square to greet the new year with a spirit of hope and unity, and the joyous atmosphere is infectious.

In summary, Seefeld's Christmas celebrations are above and above the norm, providing a unique fusion of custom, community, and wintry charm. The town's main square and Christmas markets turn into hubs of happiness and community, and the various activities and festivities give the holiday season additional layers of cultural depth.

Seefeld's Christmas is an experience that delves into the essence of Tyrolean winter magic, wherein each snowflake embodies a subtle hint of festive cheer. It's more than just a party.

WINTER ACTIVITIES: Embracing Alpine Thrills in Seefeld

Skiing and Snowboarding

Nestled in the heart of the Austrian Alps, Seefeld is a winter sports enthusiast's dream come true. It beckons those who want to experience the exhilaration of snowboarding and skiing on immaculate slopes. The town is the perfect place for both novice and experienced snowsport enthusiasts because of its proximity to top-notch ski resorts and breathtaking alpine landscapes.

For lovers of skiing, the Rosshütte ski region is a beacon. It guarantees that there is something for everyone with a variety of slopes that accommodate different ability levels, from easy beginner slopes to strenuous descents. Modern lifts take enthusiastic skiers quickly to the summit of the mountain, where breathtaking sweeping vistas await before the thrilling descent starts.

Cross-country skiing tracks winding through scenic landscapes can be found in the Leutasch Valley for those looking for a more sedate skiing experience. Seefeld's winter wonderland is seen from a different angle thanks to the peaceful environment created by the rhythmic glide of skis on groomed tracks and the crisp mountain air.

The Gschwandtkopf region is a snowboarder's paradise, with a snow park that offers obstacles for all ability levels. The design of the snowpark guarantees an exciting experience against the breathtaking Alpine backdrop, whether you're learning your first tricks or honing your most seasoned abilities.

Fun Snowshoeing Experiences

Seefeld's allure in the wintertime goes beyond the exhilaration of thrilling downhill excursions; snowshoeing excursions are open to those looking for a more sedate yet no less captivating experience. A vast network of snowshoe routes winds across stunning alpine scenery, wide fields, and forests blanketed in snow in the Olympiaregion Seefeld.

The Wildmoos region is a snowshoeing haven, with tracks suitable for all levels of fitness. The peaceful ambiance created by the snow-covered forests enables snowshoers to enjoy the majesty of unspoiled winter scenery while fostering a sense of connection with the natural world.

The Moonlight Snowshoeing Tour, which turns the midnight winter landscape into a mystical realm, is a highlight of snowshoeing in Seefeld. With the moonlight and the sound of snow crunching beneath their feet, participants follow the paths under the starry sky, making memories that will last long after the adventure is over.

Ice Skating Delights

The icy scenery of Seefeld is the perfect backdrop for magical ice skating adventures, where the crisp winter air and the rhythmic glide of skates blend. For those who enjoy ice skating, the Seefeld Ice Arena provides a central hub right in the middle of the town. A gorgeous backdrop of snow-covered trees and the landmark Seekirchl transforms the arena into a fun place for skaters of all skill levels, from leisurely spins and jumps to more technical tricks.

Visit the ice rinks that are naturally occurring across the Olympiaregion Seefeld for a more personal experience. In particular, during the winter months, Lake Wildsee becomes a vast natural ice rink. The feeling of gliding over the frozen lake while taking in the expansive views of the mountains and snow-covered beaches lends an air of fantasy to the ice skating experience.

Ice Disco Nights at the Seefeld Ice Arena allow night owls to enjoy ice skating well into the night. Skaters of all ages can dance on the ice while taking in the vibrant ambiance and friendly mood that characterize Seefeld's winter evenings under the glittering lights.

To sum up, Seefeld's winter sports provide a variety of experiences, ranging from the thrilling thrill of world-class skiing and snowboarding to the tranquil discovery of snow-covered terrain through snowshoeing expeditions. The town's wonderful ice skating adds a magical touch to the winter experience, especially when viewed against the stunning backdrop of the Alps. Seefeld invites you to experience the wonder of winter in the Austrian

Alps, whether you're looking for the peacefulness of a moonlit snowshoeing journey or the adrenaline rush of downhill descents.

DINING AND CULINARY DELIGHTS

Local Cuisine Exploration

Beyond its stunning scenery, Seefeld provides a gastronomic adventure where the deep flavors of Tyrolean cuisine entice the palate. Sophisticated recipes combined with regional ingredients and traditional Alpine meals make for a filling and decadent dining experience.

Start your journey with a taste of **Käsespätzle**, a savory treat that combines Alpine cheese with handmade noodles to create an incredibly delicious combination of flavors and textures. This meal epitomizes the heartiness of Tyrolean cuisine, and it's typically served with crispy onions that give every bite a delightful crunch.

Try the traditional Tyrolean dish **Hirschbraten mit Preiselbeeren (roast venison with**

lingonberries) for a taste of the local game. The region's affinity to its natural surroundings is reflected in the symphony of flavors created by the soft, juicy flesh and the sweet, tangy lingonberries.

Enjoying **Tiroler Gröstl** is a must-do when exploring Tyrolean cuisine. This warm and delectable savory mélange is made with potatoes, onions, and leftover meats in a hearty pan-fried dish. The quintessential Alpine comfort meal, Tiroler Gröstl is typically consumed with a fried egg on top.

Seefeld is home to several mountain huts, or "**hütten**," where you may get a true taste of the native cuisine. These rustic enterprises provide spectacular vistas, a warm atmosphere, and delicious food. In the stunning Tyrolean Alps, savor a hot cup of Kaspressknödel soup or a filling plate of Alm Butterbrot.

Christmas-Themed Dining Experiences

Seefeld's dining experiences take on a festive twist, embracing the spirit of the holidays as the restaurant turns into a winter wonderland during the Christmas season. There are several dining establishments with a Christmas theme that combine classic cuisines with delicious seasonal fare to enhance the festive spirit.

During the holidays, several Seefeld's eateries and hütten serve unique Christmas menus that highlight the best Tyrolean food with a festive flair. Anticipate recipes that are enhanced by seasonal components such as cranberries, chestnuts, and fragrant spices, resulting in a harmonious blend of tastes that evoke the coziness of the holiday season.

Enjoy a Christmas Eve feast, a centuries-old Tyrolean custom when friends and family get together to celebrate with a spectacular dinner. In a warm, festive setting, local restaurants frequently provide unique Christmas Eve meals that offer a sense of the culinary legacy of the area.

Consider going to a Tyrolean Christmas Dinner Show for a distinctive Christmas eating experience. Delicious holiday feasts are served at these gatherings together with live performances of traditional Tyrolean music and dancing. The festive mood and the delicious smells of holiday fare combine to produce a memorable evening that combines cuisine and cultural celebration.

Cozy Bakeries and Cafés
Seefeld's charming bakeries and cafés beckon guests to relax and indulge in delicious sweets during the bitter cold of winter. These restaurants offer a sanctuary for individuals in search of a break from outdoor exploration, with their alpine-inspired décor and welcoming aroma of freshly baked pastries.

Visit one of Seefeld's charming cafés to begin your day and savor a leisurely breakfast and hot cups of scented coffee. Savor freshly made pastries, like decadent strudels and buttery croissants, to set the stage for an ideal day of discovery.

Seefeld's cafés are magical during the Christmas season when many of them have festive décor and sweets just for the occasion. Enjoy a slice of Stollen, a traditional German fruit cake enhanced with nuts, dried fruits, and flavorful spices, or stay warm with a cup of spiced Christmas tea. Cafés are transformed into holiday cheer havens with their festive offerings.

Experience the skill of Tyrolean bakers as they create a range of traditional and seasonal treats by stopping by a neighborhood bakery. Snack on a slice of Linzer Torte, a traditional Austrian pastry with a lattice-topped buttery dough filled with raspberry jam. A delightful delicacy ideal for a cozy afternoon treat is created by the fusion of sweet, tangy, and nutty ingredients.

Discover the Nordic Bakery in Seefeld, which is well-known for its Scandinavian-inspired pastries, for a distinctive café experience. Enjoy treats that have been flavored with cinnamon, such as Swedish cinnamon buns, and take in the calm atmosphere that will take you to a peaceful winter hideaway in the North.

In summary, Seefeld's culinary scene entices guests to go on a gustatory adventure, ranging from the hearty flavors of classic Tyrolean cuisine to the joyful sensations of Christmas-themed dining establishments. Warm bakeries and cafés provide a touch of coziness and charm, making them the ideal places to relax and indulge in the delectable treats that characterize this Alpine gem's winter cuisine.

SHOPPING GUIDE: Unveiling Seefeld's Winter Treasures

Unique Christmas Gifts

Seefeld provides a shopping experience that is above and above the norm with its quaint cobblestone streets and Alpine charm. The town comes alive with a festive atmosphere when winter descends upon it, and the boutiques and shops entice with distinctive Christmas items that capture the essence of the season.

Look through the local businesses that feature Tyrolean artisans' handicrafts for unique Christmas gifts. Among the riches awaiting discovery are locally produced textiles, hand-carved wooden ornaments, and elaborately crafted glassware. These custom pieces are timeless keepsakes of Seefeld's winter magic in addition to being kind presents.

Savor the charm of Seefeld's Christmas markets, where a variety of handcrafted goods are available from wooden stalls decorated with sparkling lights. Find locally made jams and honey, classic Tyrolean hats, and hand-knit woolen garments. The markets offer a fully immersive shopping experience, enabling patrons to engage in conversation with craftspeople and discover the narratives underlying each handcrafted item.

Think about choosing bespoke presents from Seefeld's upscale jewelry boutiques. Local jewelers frequently use Alpine-inspired patterns in their pieces; examples include pendants with mountain images and earrings with snowy themes. These classic pieces are treasured presents for loved ones because they perfectly express Seefeld's inherent beauty.

Local Artisan Markets

The lively artisan markets that are scattered around Seefeld demonstrate the town's dedication to maintaining its cultural legacy and provide a window into the creative energy of the area. These marketplaces give regional craftspeople a stage on which to display their abilities, resulting in a genuine and educational purchasing experience.

Seasonal artisan markets honoring the richness of Tyrolean workmanship are held in the Olympiaregion Seefeld. Wander among the booths featuring artisanal woodworking, textile art, and pottery. Talk to the craftspeople; a lot of them are eager to share the history and methods that go into their creations.

Explore the Seekirchen Christmas Market, which is situated in front of the famous Seekirche. This market encourages guests to discover Seefeld's rich creative history with its lively atmosphere and well chosen assortment of crafts. The market offers a plethora of one-of-a-kind treasures, ranging from locally manufactured chocolates to hand-painted ceramics.

Don't pass up the chance to tour Seefeld's glass blowing workshops. Here, talented artists create beautiful objects out of molten glass, from useful glassware to delicate decorations. Seeing the glass treasures up close adds a level of appreciation that makes them even more special as gifts or mementos.

Souvenirs to Remember

To help tourists take a piece of this winter wonderland home with them, Seefeld provides a variety of souvenirs that capture the essence of the town's Alpine beauty. Think of choosing mementos that perfectly convey Seefeld's natural beauty and cultural legacy.

Cozy woolen scarves and embroidered mittens are two examples of Tyrolean textiles that make for fashionable and useful mementos. Local stores provide a wide range of designs, many of which are based on classic Alpine themes. These products serve as wearing mementos of Seefeld's eternal attractiveness in addition to offering warmth during the winter.

Look for books that explore the rich history and culture of the Tyrolean region in the town's booksellers. These literary gems, which range from exquisitely illustrated coffee table books to educational guides on the Alpine scenery, provide a greater insight of Seefeld's history and make thoughtful mementos.

Indulge in locally made chocolates and confections as a delightful memento of your time in Seefeld. The town's chocolatiers take great delight in crafting delicious confections that frequently feature local flavors utilizing premium ingredients. These candies, which come in adorable boxes with Alpine designs, are perfect as gifts or as indulgences for yourself.

Discover festive decorations and ornaments that capture the essence of the season in Seefeld's Christmas markets. Choose from items like hand-blown glass decorations, wooden tree ornaments, and elaborately carved candles to infuse your holiday décor with a little of Seefeld's wintry charm.

To sum up, Seefeld's shopping guide takes you on a tour of the town's cultural and artistic gems. Handmade Christmas items that capture the spirit of Tyrolean craftsmanship can be found at neighborhood businesses and Christmas markets. Discovering the skills of Seefeld's creative community can be gained by perusing the area's artisan markets. Carefully chosen souvenirs become enduring keepsakes that capture the allure of the alpine setting and the enchantment of the winter season in this charming location.

ENTERTAINMENT AND NIGHTLIFE:
Revelry Amidst Alpine Splendor

Evening Shows and Performances

Known for its daytime Alpine adventures, Seefeld effortlessly transforms into a nightlife and evening entertainment destination, providing a wide range of events and acts to suit all interests.

The Casino Seefeld is a glimmer of excitement in the evening, beckoning guests to try their luck in an elegant setting. In addition to games, the casino regularly hosts events including themed parties and live music performances. It's a location where the allure of the surroundings blends with the excitement of the game to create a fully immersive evening experience.

Explore **the Pfarrkirche St. Oswald**, the town's major parish church, for a cultural evening. There are frequently classical concerts presented there. This old church's acoustics provide for an exquisite venue for events, from chamber music recitals to symphony concerts. Every musical experience is enhanced by the ethereal atmosphere created by the warm glow of candles.

Seefeld often hosts evening shows that celebrate the arts of the theater. Look through the local event calendar to see what's happening at places like the Congress and Exhibition Centre. You may catch anything from modern productions to classic Tyrolean plays onstage. These performances, which frequently have a cultural or seasonal focus, provide an engrossing fusion of entertainment and cultural immersion.

Festive Bars and Pubs

Seefeld's clubs and taverns come alive as the sun sets over the Tyrolean Alps, providing a lively nightlife scene that suits a variety of tastes and moods. The town's busy pubs and bars offer the ideal setting for evening celebrations, whether you're looking for a warm place to chat or a vibrant place to dance.

In Seefeld, traditional Tyrolean pubs known as 'Tiroler Stube' offer a taste of local libations. These homey, rustic places serve you local wines, schnapps, and beers while radiating warmth and charm. Talk to people in the area over a strong beer, and you'll discover that these places are gathering places for more than simply libations.

Seefeld's pubs frequently take on festive themes as Christmas draws near, complete with garlands, sparkling lights, and holiday-themed beverages. These locations' ambient lighting creates a joyous atmosphere that makes them the perfect place to celebrate the season with friends and fellow travelers.

Visit Seefeld's cocktail bars for an introduction to global cuisines, while talented mixologists create inventive cocktails. In stylish and contemporary settings, enjoy masterfully prepared martinis, creative seasonal cocktails, and timeless classics. The cocktail bars frequently include DJ sets or live music, which enhances the atmosphere and tempts patrons to stay out late dancing.

Nighttime Strolls

Seefeld's allure lingerie late into the evening, beckoning guests to take strolls into the night to take in the serenity of the town's winter scenery and its sparkling splendor.

The town center is the ideal location for an evening stroll that is both romantic and reflective because of the glittering lights and the glow of the storefronts. Take in the silence of the winter night as the streets coated in snow sparkle in the gentle light of the street lamps.

Wander the paths surrounding Lake Wildsee, where the tranquil and alluring sight is created by the moonlight reflecting off the frozen surface. The fresh night air and the shadows cast by the nearby mountains add to the charm of the promenade. This is an opportunity to enjoy the serenity and untainted beauty that characterize Seefeld after dark.

Take a guided torchlight hike for a more daring midnight experience. Participants walk down snowy routes beneath a starry sky, creating a magnificent procession with flickering torches. These guided excursions offer a distinctive and engaging way to enjoy Seefeld's winter nights, with stops frequently made for astronomy or storytelling.

Seefeld's enchanted winter landscape reaches the town's periphery, where moonlit woodlands and meadows assume an enchanted aura. Think about going on a guided snowshoeing excursion at night, where you may explore the Alpine sceneries while enjoying the satisfying crunch of snow beneath your feet. Long after the journey is over, you'll still feel the surreal atmosphere created by the stillness of the night and the twinkling of the stars.

To sum up, Seefeld's nightlife and entertainment options appeal to a variety of tastes, from nighttime theatergoers to partygoers searching for lively pubs and clubs. Take a stroll at night to enjoy the tranquil beauty and enchanted charm that Seefeld radiates, whether it's in the town center, near Lake Wildsee, or through landscapes blanketed in snow. As night falls, Seefeld becomes a nocturnal paradise where natural beauty and entertainment blend in the heart of Tyrol's Alps.

FAMILY-FRIENDLY ACTIVITIES: Winter Adventures for All Ages in Seefeld

Kid-Friendly Winter Fun

Seefeld welcomes families with open arms and offers a plethora of family-friendly winter activities that transform the wintry scenery into an imaginative playground. The town makes sure that every family member, regardless of age, may enjoy the magic of the season, from markets to slopes blanketed in snow.

With designated kid-friendly zones and ski schools, the Rosshütte ski area welcomes even the smallest travelers. These areas are made to let children experience the fun and safety of skiing for the first time. Children are guided through the fundamentals by qualified instructors, who are frequently adept at making learning enjoyable. This builds their confidence on the slopes.

Seefeld has family-friendly toboggan runs for people looking for a new kind of downhill fun. A well-kept toboggan track offers an exhilarating fall through meadows covered with snow in the Gschwandtkopf area. Local toboggan rentals are available for families, guaranteeing a fun-filled day of shared memories and laughter as everyone zooms down the hill.

A quick drive from Seefeld brings you to the Leutasch Valley, a winter wonderland ideal for leisurely hiking and family outings. Together, parents and kids can explore the enchanted woodland as the well-maintained, level paths meander through the snow-covered patches. This is an occasion to take in the splendor of the Tyrolean Alps and spend valuable time with your family.

Encounters with Santa Claus

During the Christmas season, Seefeld becomes a storybook setting, and what better way to win over young hearts than seeing Santa Claus himself? Families make treasured memories as the community crafts joyful events that bring Santa's magic to life.

Visit the Christmas markets in Seefeld, where Santa frequently makes surprise appearances and delights kids with his cheerful presence. Little ones get to wish the man in the red suit a happy Christmas season and these interactions make for ideal photo ops. The marketplaces transform into a site of joyous celebration, as Santa brings happiness to both residents and tourists.

Take into consideration going to one of the town's Santa Claus parades for an immersive experience. In these brightly lit processions, Santa Claus is accompanied by jovial elves and celebratory figures as he makes his way through the streets. A captivating enchanted environment is created by the parades, which frequently feature dance, music, and the distribution of candies, captivating spectators of all ages.

Certain local establishments host special Santa Claus-themed activities to offer an extra bit of magic. These entertaining and creative events, which range from interactive workshops to storytelling sessions, let kids get into the holiday spirit. When planning your stay, keep an eye on the local event calendar for information about Santa Claus sightings and related events.

Ideas for Family Bonding

Seefeld recognizes the value of family time and offers a setting for fostering enduring bonds and shared experiences among its picturesque winter scenery. Families can spend a variety of times together in the town, whether it be through festive traditions, outdoor exploration, or participation in winter sports.

A family-friendly horse-drawn carriage ride throughout Seefeld's surrounding winter splendor is something to consider. A peaceful rhythm is created by the soft clip-clop of hooves as you curl up under warm blankets. Families may enjoy the stunning Alpine views and make memories together by taking advantage of the carriage rides, which frequently include pauses at picturesque viewpoints.

For hikers of all ages, the Olympiaregion Seefeld offers a vast network of winter hiking routes. Take a family walk through enchanted woodlands and snow-covered meadows while layering up in warm clothing. To improve the experience for young explorers, several trails have interactive features like themed hikes or environmental discoveries.

Seefeld's ice skating options are part of its family-friendly vibe. Come to the Seefeld Ice Arena to enjoy a joyful skating experience for both adults and children. To create an inclusive atmosphere where everyone may experience the thrill of ice skating, the arena frequently conducts special events including family skating sessions.

Seefeld's creative workshops are a fun way for families with young artists to connect while fostering an exploration of artistic expression. These crafts and pottery classes, which have holiday themes, provide both parents and kids with an enjoyable and interactive experience. If you're visiting, ask the organizers about forthcoming family-friendly programs at the art studios or events around town.

In conclusion, Seefeld offers family-friendly activities that accommodate a range of ages and interests. The town makes sure that families may enjoy the beauty of the season, offering everything from kid-friendly winter activities on the slopes to magical sightings of Santa Claus that delight young hearts. In the middle of Seefeld's snowy surroundings, family-friendly activities like carriage rides, winter treks, or creative workshops offer chances for connection and happiness.

PRACTICAL TIPS FOR A MERRY VISIT TO SEEFELD'S WINTER WONDERLAND

Weather and Clothing Recommendations

Seefeld's winter weather, with its snowy vistas and clean Alpine air, demands careful planning in terms of attire and readiness. Here are some advice regarding the weather and attire to make your visit pleasant:

Layering Is Crucial: Since temperatures can change during the day, wearing layers of clothing enables you to adapt to the changing weather. To stay dry, start with a base layer that wicks away moisture, put on an insulating layer for warmth, and finish with an outer layer that is windproof and waterproof.

Warm Accessories: The significance of accessories should not be overlooked. Thermal socks, a warm hat, and well-insulated gloves are necessities for staying warm. For an added layer of comfort when participating in outdoor activities, think about bringing hand warmers.

Waterproof Footwear: Your best friend when there's snow on the ground is waterproof boots. To keep your feet toasty and dry while exploring Seefeld's winter wonderland, go with insulated boots.

Snow Gear: Make sure you have the right equipment if you're going to participate in winter activities. To further defend against snow and wind, wear goggles, a waterproof jacket, and snow pants.

Examine the Weather Forecast: Throughout your visit, be aware of the expected weather. Seefeld sees a range of winter conditions, so planning and dressing accordingly can help you get the most out of your visit.

Language and Communication Tips

Seefeld is a friendly place where both locals and tourists from other countries congregate. Even if many locals are multilingual and speak English, following a few language and communication pointers will improve your visit overall:

Learn Some fundamental Phrases: Since German is the most common language in Seefeld, become familiar with some fundamental German phrases. When attempting to establish a connection with locals, basic greetings, courteous expressions, and everyday inquiries can be very helpful.

Employ a Translation tool: To overcome linguistic barriers, think about utilizing a translation tool. When interacting with menus, signage, or conversations where linguistic discrepancies may occur, these techniques can be helpful.

Accept bilingual Signs: Seefeld, a well-liked vacation spot, frequently has bilingual signs. Nonetheless, knowing the typical terminology used in German for amenities, services, and directions is useful.

Friendly Gestures: Despite language problems, nonverbal cues like smiles and gestures can convey meaning. Seefeld's citizens are used to engaging with outsiders, thus being amiable can help build strong bonds.

Local Pronunciations: Although English is commonly spoken, locals can appreciate an effort to pronounce names and locations in German. It puts a personal touch on your relationships and demonstrates a certain amount of cultural respect.

Precautions for Safety

Seefeld places a high priority on the security and welfare of its guests. These safety measures are important to remember to guarantee a worry-free and secure experience:

Winter Sports Safety: Respect safety regulations and stay on approved routes if you intend to participate in winter sports like skiing or snowboarding. Always wear the proper safety equipment, such as helmets, and keep your ability level in mind.

Snow Conditions Awareness: Keep yourself updated about the state of the snow, particularly if you want to venture into off-piste territory. When heading into backcountry terrain, it is advisable to check local advisories and carry the proper equipment because avalanche safety is very important.

Emergency Contacts: Learn the names and numbers of medical institutions, embassies, and consulates that are closest to you. Give your traveling buddies access to these phone numbers by storing them in your phone.

Winter Driving Precautions: Be ready for the state of the roads if you intend to drive while you're here. Make sure your car has snow tires, and make sure you have an emergency kit, an ice scraper, and a shovel on you. Become familiar with the rules governing local traffic.

Sun protection and Hydration: It's crucial to stay hydrated, especially if you're exercising, even in the chilly weather. Furthermore, use sunscreen and sunglasses to protect your skin and eyes from the sun's strong reflection on snow.

COVID-19 Guidelines: During your visit, be aware of any specific COVID-19 guidelines or restrictions that may be in effect. To protect yourself and others, abide by local laws, observe social distancing protocols, and wear masks in authorized places.

Finally, these useful suggestions are meant to improve your trip to Seefeld and create a joyful and unforgettable experience. You may truly immerse yourself in the enchanted winter wonderland that Seefeld offers by dressing appropriately for the weather, accepting linguistic considerations, and putting safety first.

DAY TRIPS AND EXCURSIONS: Exploring Beyond Seefeld's Winter Magic

Nearby Attractions

Seefeld's allure goes beyond its scenes blanketed in snow; it serves as a springboard to neighboring sites that enhance and diversify your winter vacation. The following local sights are worth visiting and would be interesting day trips:

The Alpine Capital: From Seefeld, it's a short drive to Innsbruck, the capital of Tyrol, a city rich in architectural grandeur and history. Take a trip around the quaint Old Town, see the Golden Roof, and investigate the Imperial Palace. Situated in Innsbruck, the fascinating Swarovski Crystal Worlds Museum showcases the creativity of crystal.

Garmisch-Partenkirchen: Discover the charming town of Garmisch-Partenkirchen, set against the backdrop of the Bavarian Alps, by traveling across the border into Germany. Not far away is Germany's tallest peak, the Zugspitze. A lovely combination of historic landmarks, alpine charm, and winter sports activities can be found in Garmisch-Partenkirchen.

Mittenwald: A Harmony of Shades: Mittenwald is a charming village encircled by snow-capped peaks, well-known for its vividly painted houses and rich musical heritage. Wander slowly along its cobblestone streets, stop by the museum dedicated to violin-making, and soak in the charming ambiance of this hidden gem of a Bavarian town.

Ettal Abbey: Spiritual Serenity: If you're looking for a quiet getaway, think about paying a visit to Ettal Abbey, a 14th-century Benedictine monastery.

A peaceful environment for reflection and discovery is created by the elaborate interior of the monastery, the tranquil grounds, and the neighboring Ettal Alps.

Beyond Seefeld Adventure

Seefeld's advantageous location makes it possible to embark on thrilling excursions outside of the town limits, each of which provides a distinctive viewpoint of the Alpine scenery:

The Jewel of the Alps, Nordkette:
The breathtaking mountain range known as the Nordkette, sometimes called the Jewel of the Alps, is reachable after a quick drive to Innsbruck. From Innsbruck, the Hungerburgbahn funicular transports you to Hungerburg, from where the Nordkette Cable Car continues its ascent to the Hafelekar mountain. Savor expansive vistas of the

Tyrolean Alps, and winter trekking paths await the most daring.

Zugspitze - Bavaria's Summit: Take an exciting day excursion to Germany's highest peak, Zugspitze, which offers unmatched views of the surrounding peaks. Reachable via a charming cogwheel train or cable car, the peak offers an amazing view of the Alps. For those looking for alpine thrills, the Zugspitze provides skiing and snowboarding chances throughout the winter.

Leutasch Gorge: A Masterwork of Nature
A short drive from Seefeld, explore the Leutasch Gorge's natural splendor. The River Ache sculpted the gorge's route, which leads past spectacular rock formations and glimpses of ice waterfalls. The gorge is a perfect place for a quiet stroll in the middle of nature during the winter months when it becomes a tranquil winter wonderland.

Visit the Partnach Gorge, which is close to Garmisch-Partenkirchen, where the gorge is transformed into a captivating exhibit of ice sculptures throughout the winter months. Stroll through the ice wonderland, which is encircled by craggy rocks that have frozen waterfalls on them. A leisurely winter stroll or a gorgeous horse-drawn carriage ride will easily take you to the gorge.

Scenic Drives

Beautiful drives that showcase the Austrian and Bavarian Alps' stunning grandeur may be found all around Seefeld. Take your camera with you and go out on these beautiful adventures:

Arlberg Pass - Alpine Majesty: Take a picturesque journey through the magnificent Arlberg mountain range as you begin the Arlberg Pass drive. You pass across frozen lakes, snow-covered forests, and quaint villages. The picturesque landscapes, particularly those near the Flexen Pass, present an exquisite display of Alpine majesty.

Silvretta High Alpine Road - Alpine Splendor: Visit the Silvretta High Alpine Road for an amazing road trip. This scenic path winds through the mountain range of the Silvretta, offering breathtaking vistas of snow-capped peaks and glistening alpine lakes. The route offers an incredible adventure into the heart of the Austrian Alps, but it is frequently blocked in the winter.

Romantic Road: Enchanting Villages: Travel through the charming Bavarian villages along the Romantic Road, a historic road. The entire journey is lengthy, but parts of it near Seefeld pass through quaint towns like Füssen, which is famous for the majestic Neuschwanstein Castle. For those looking for a romantic winter getaway, the drive is a wonderful trip that gives glimpses of fairytale landscapes.

Alpine Vineyards on the Tyrolean Wine Road: This wine country charm is combined with alpine splendor. This charming journey passes through orchards and vineyards with snow-capped mountains in the background. Savor regional wines, visit nearby wineries, and take in the tranquil atmosphere of this one-of-a-kind Tyrolean experience.

Finally, Seefeld offers day tours and excursions that encourage you to discover the various landscapes and cultural gems that surround this gem of the Alps. Whether you go into nearby towns, climb mountains, or take scenic drives, every trip is sure to add fresh viewpoints and life-changing experiences to your winter travels.

LOCAL INSIGHTS: Seefeld Unveiled through Interviews and Christmas Stories

Interviews with Seefeld Residents

We look to the locals themselves, whose lives are deeply entwined with the fabric of this Alpine town, to fully comprehend the pulse of Seefeld. We learn a great deal about their viewpoints, experiences, and the special charm that makes Seefeld through a series of interviews.

Local Artist Klaus: Through his work as a proficient woodcarver, Klaus expresses his love for maintaining Tyrolean traditions. "Woodcarving is a means of preserving our past, not just a job. Every item narrates a tale about the Alps, our past, and the relationship between the environment and our neighborhood. It's a pleasure to tell visitors about the cultural significance of the carvings since they frequently inquire about them."

Maria, a Hütten Hostess: Offering a window into the hearty hospitality of Tyrolean hospitality, Maria manages a traditional mountain hut. "People congregate, laugh, and share in our hütte. The smell of mulled wine permeates the air as the fire crackles in the winter. It's a comfortable haven for both locals and tourists. What makes it unique is witnessing families and friends creating memories here."

Ski Instructor Sebastian: Experienced ski instructor Sebastian emphasizes the delight of instructing winter sports in Seefeld. Here, skiing is a way of life rather than just a sport. It's quite satisfying to teach adults and kids how to handle the slopes safely. The enchantment of Seefeld itself is reflected in the twinkle in their eyes after they complete a run. It's about embracing the Alpine spirit, not just about skill."

Personal Stories of Christmas in Seefeld

Seefeld experiences a mystical metamorphosis as the winter months progress, and anecdotes from Christmastime personal narratives encapsulate the spirit of this enchanted period.

The Christmas Eve Tradition of the Müller Family: The Müller family, who have lived in Seefeld for a long time, reveals their treasured custom. "We get together for the candlelight service at the Seekirchen once a year. With the church lit up against the snowy background, a calm ambiance is created. We then take a stroll through the village covered in snow to our preferred hütte, where we exchange little gifts and enjoy a joyful supper. We are connected to Seefeld's neighborhood and the wonder of Christmas through this custom."

An International Christmas Story: The Smith family from the United States is one of the tourists who fall in love with Seefeld and discover the town over the holidays. "We didn't intend to spend Christmas in Seefeld, but we were enthralled by the little town and its wintry scenery. We sampled traditional Tyrolean sweets, went ice skating with the locals, and joined them at the Christmas market. Our family will always cherish the unexpected, magical Christmas that transpired."

The Story of Helena's Winter Wedding: A resident of Seefeld, Helena has happy memories of her winter wedding in the town. Seefeld is gorgeous in the winter, which is why it was the ideal location for our wedding. With snowflakes softly falling all around us, we exchanged vows, and our guests celebrated with a celebratory meal in a hütte with a view of the snow-covered surroundings. Our wonderful day had a touch of a fairytale thanks to Seefeld's winter magic."

Seefeld's residents and visitors alike show a town profoundly entwined with its traditions, the joy of winter activities, and the enchantment of Christmas in these personal anecdotes and interviews. The voices of those who live in Seefeld and those who visit its beauties bring the town's character to life, whether it is via the deft hands of artisans, the coziness of mountain huts, the excitement of skiing, or the charm of holiday customs.

SEEFELD ON A BUDGET: Unveiling Affordable Delights in the Alpine Haven

Free and Low-Cost Attractions

Seefeld, tucked away in the Austrian Alps, may radiate luxury, but it also throws out its arms to travelers on a tight budget. Explore the town's captivating features at no cost or minimal cost by making use of these attractions:

Nature's Splendor at No Cost: Seefeld's most valuable asset is its astounding natural beauty, which is freely accessible. Take a stroll around the town's quaint streets, which are bordered by gorgeous scenery and snow-capped mountains. A short drive away, the Leutasch Valley has free winter walking routes so you may enjoy the pure Alpine landscape without spending a single dime.

Discover famous sites like Seekirchl, the quaint church tucked up against the Alps, by taking a walking tour of the Olympic Rings. Spend no money and take in the serene surroundings and architecture. The Olympic Rings, which honor Seefeld's role in hosting the Winter Olympics, are located nearby and provide an ideal location for a special picture.

Free Winter Activities: Take advantage of winter sports without breaking the bank. Cross-country skiing routes in Seefeld are free of charge and suitable for both novices and experts. Pack your gear or rent reasonably priced items from nearby stores. Affordable ice skating is encouraged on frozen lakes, such as Wildsee, which offers a mystical experience without breaking the bank.

Affordable Eateries

Enjoy delicious food without breaking the bank by checking out Seefeld's selection of reasonably priced restaurants, which combine regional specialties with cost-effective options:

Tyrolean Bäckerei Delight: Begin your day by stopping by one of Seefeld's historic bakeries. These undiscovered treasures provide reasonably priced freshly baked foods, ranging from fluffy pastries to substantial bread. Snack on a warm pretzel or a strudel packed with cheese while you stroll about the village and experience true Tyrolean sensations without going over your budget.

Local Hütten with Inexpensive Bites: Seefeld's hütten, or mountain huts, provide affordable options in addition to après-ski enjoyment. Choose filling soups, classic käsespätzle (cheese noodles), or a big serving of goulash. Tastes of Tyrolean cuisine are offered in these mountain resorts, at prices that won't lighten your pocketbook.

Coffee Lovers' Marketplatz Cafés: The quaint Marktplatz (**market square**) is home to welcoming cafés where you may relax without going over budget. Savor a slice of freshly made cake or a cup of delicious Austrian coffee while admiring the beautiful surroundings. Many of the cafés have outdoor seating, so you can take in the ambiance for a reasonable price.

Food Markets for Local Delights: For a cheap yet genuine dining experience, check out Seefeld's food markets. Local producers, cheeses, and refreshments are displayed by the sellers. Gather some locally produced cheeses, fresh fruit, and a baguette for an inexpensive picnic at one of Seefeld's picturesque locations. It's a delicious way to savor regional cuisine without having to pay for restaurant dining.

Budget - Friendly Accommodation

Seefeld offers a selection of reasonably priced lodging choices that let you relax and revive without sacrificing comfort:

Pensions and Guesthouses: Take in Seefeld's homey charm while you stay in these various types of accommodations. These cozy, family-run lodgings are frequently more reasonably priced than larger hotels and have a welcoming atmosphere. Savor attentive service and cozy accommodations while staying within your means.

Seefeld is home to several inexpensive hotels and hostels that are ideal for the astute tourist. With the simple yet clean amenities these lodgings offer, you may spend more of your money touring the town and its environs. Seek accommodations that are conveniently close to Seefeld's top attractions.

Vacation Rentals: If you're planning a group trip or a prolonged stay, you might want to think about renting a vacation apartment. With the freedom to cook your meals and snacks, these self-catering solutions help you save down on eating costs. Make use of the conveniences of home while traveling and properly manage your money.

Discounts for Off-Peak and Midweek Stays: Make the most of your money by thinking about off-peak and midweek stays. Seefeld Lodging frequently has deals during off-peak times, so you may enjoy the town's beauty without having to pay peak-season prices. To get the greatest deals, look for exclusive offers and flexible booking options.

Budget travel to Seefeld is not only an option, but an invitation to see the town's treasures without worrying about money. Seefeld welcomes visitors looking for Alpine charm without breaking the bank with activities for free in the outdoors, reasonably priced dining options, and lodging options that fit any budget. In this charming winter paradise, embrace the charm of the Austrian Alps without going over budget.

A MAGICAL CHRISTMAS IN SEEFELD: Sample Itinerary to Embrace the Festive Spirit

Day 1: Arrival and Welcome to Winter Wonderland

Morning

When you get to Seefeld, check into your comfortable lodging. Explore the quaint alleyways of the snow-covered town on a leisurely morning stroll while taking in the festive mood.

Afternoon

Visit your neighborhood bakery to have a typical Austrian pastry or snack. In one of the cozy cafés on Marktplatz, indulge in a steaming hot chocolate or scented coffee to warm up.

Evening

Take a guided walking tour of Seefeld's Christmas lights and decorations as the sun sets. Festive displays bring the town to life and create a mystical atmosphere.

Day 2: Discover the Magical Holiday Markets

Morning

Get your day started at a nearby guesthouse or café with a substantial Tyrolean breakfast. Take in the serene beauty of the surrounding area by visiting the Seekirchen, the famous church set against the snow-capped Alps.

Afternoon

Experience the joyous atmosphere of Seefeld's Christmas markets. Explore booths filled with locally made goods, ornaments, and one-of-a-kind presents. To lift your spirits, sip on a cup of fragrant mulled wine, or Glühwein.

Evening

Enjoy the cuisine of the town at one of the hüttes. Savor a traditional Tyrolean supper of substantial goulash or käsespätzle, or cheese noodles. Bask in the warm atmosphere of the mountain cabin, which is enhanced by the glow of the fireplace and flickering candles.

Day 3: Alpine Charm and Winter Adventures

Morning

Prepare for wintertime pursuits. To fully experience the beautiful Alpine scenery, choose between going on a guided snowshoeing tour or exploring the cross-country skiing paths.

Afternoon

Stop for lunch at a nearby restaurant. To refuel for your afternoon travels, try a classic schnitzel or a bowl of robust soup.

Evening

Indulge in a spa treatment at one of Seefeld's wellness centers as the day comes to an end. After a day of winter exploration, unwind with a peaceful massage or in a sauna.

Day 4: Day Trip to Nearby Attractions

Morning

Take a day excursion to some neighboring sights. Pick between the vibrant culture of Innsbruck and the quaint town of Mittenwald, which is well-known for its painted buildings. Take in the local food, visit the museums, and explore the sites.

Afternoon

Take a stroll around the town square and stop by any local shops or marketplaces. Get mementos or unusual Christmas presents to bring a little bit of the charm of the Alps home.

Evening

Go back to Seefeld and have a nice meal at a restaurant serving Tyrolean cuisine. Savor the local cuisine and raise a glass to the memories made throughout your joyous vacation.

Day 5: Culinary Delights and Farewell

Morning

Savor a leisurely breakfast as you bid farewell to your Alpine hideaway. Think about stopping by a nearby artisan market to find one-of-a-kind handcrafted gems.

Afternoon

Take a cooking class to cap off your Seefeld Christmas experience. Learn how to make Tyrolean foods like Kletzenbrot or Schlutzkrapfen. Savor the results of your efforts with a celebratory lunch.

Evening

Take one more walk through the lit streets of Seefeld before saying goodbye. Take in the spirit of the Alpine paradise one final time before returning home and bringing the coziness of Seefeld's Christmas with you.

This suggested schedule perfectly encapsulates the spirit of a mystical Christmas in Seefeld, fusing joyous customs, wintry explorations, and delectable cuisine to forge enduring memories deep inside the Austrian Alps.

CONCLUSION: A Winter Wonderland Farewell from Seefeld

Your trip through winter ends as the snowflakes dance across the little village of Seefeld and the sounds of celebration remain. Seefeld makes a lasting impression on you with its charming Christmas spirit and the attraction of the Alps.

Every moment you spent in Seefeld, whether you were exploring the glistening markets, trying out some winter sports, or just enjoying the regional specialties, added to the whole experience.

Take with you the coziness of mountain cottages and snow-covered scenery, along with the warmth and charm of a Seefeld Christmas, as you bid farewell to these places. The Alpine embrace from Seefeld is a treasured memory till the next winter trip.

COOKING UP SEEFELD CHRISTMAS DELIGHTS: Festive Recipes from the Alpine Wonderland

The delightful smell of holiday delicacies permeates the air as snowfall falls upon Seefeld, a quaint hamlet that epitomizes the spirit of Christmas. Using these beautiful and original recipes inspired by the Alpine splendor, you can bring the warmth and flavors of Seefeld into your own home.

1. Tyrolean Glühwein (Mulled Wine)

Ingredients
One 750 ml bottle of red wine
One orange, chopped
8 cloves and 1 lemon, sliced
two sticks of cinnamon
one-star anise
Three tablespoons of sugar (adjust to taste)
1 cup of water

Instructions

Put the water, sugar, orange, and lemon slices, and stir them together in a pot.

Stir in star anise, cloves, and cinnamon sticks.

Simmer the mixture while heating it over medium heat. Simmer for five to ten minutes to allow the flavors to seep in.

After adding the red wine, slowly warm the blend. Take caution not to overheat.

After it's heated, drain the mulled wine to get rid of the citrus segments and spices.

Garnish the Tyrolean Glühwein with a cinnamon stick or an orange slice and serve it in mugs.

With every warm sip, this festive mulled wine evokes the spirit of Seefeld's Christmas markets and creates a pleasant ambiance.

2. Kletzenbrot (Dried Pear Bread)

Ingredients

1 cup chopped dried figs, 1 cup chopped dried
pears, and 1 cup chopped raisins
One cup of chopped nuts (hazelnuts or walnuts)
and two cups of all-purpose flour
A smidgeon of baking powder
one tsp finely ground cinnamon
one-half tsp ground cloves
One-half tsp ground nutmeg
Half a teaspoon of salt
1 cup of honey
half a cup of milk

Instructions

Set oven temperature to 325°F, or 160°C. Oil and
dust a loaf pan.

Put the nuts, raisins, dried figs, and dried pears in a big basin.

Mix the flour, baking powder, nutmeg, cloves, cinnamon, and salt in a different basin.

Heat the milk and honey in a saucepan over low heat until thoroughly mixed.

After whisking to coat, pour the honey and milk mixture over the nuts and dried fruit.

Stirring until thoroughly blended, gradually add the dry ingredients to the fruit mixture.

After preheating the loaf pan, pour the batter into it and level the top.

Once a toothpick put into the center comes out clean, bake for one to one and a half hours.

When slicing, let the Kletzenbrot cool.

Seefeld's holiday season is embodied in the sweet and hearty delight known as Kletzenbrot, a typical Tyrolean dried pear bread.

3. Tiroler Schlutzkrapfen (Tyrolean Dumplings)

Ingredients

For the Dough

Two cups of flour (all-purpose)
Two big eggs
half a cup of water
Salt, 1/2 tsp, for the filling

One cup of cooked and mashed potatoes
One cup of boiled and chopped spinach
Half a cup of ricotta
Grated Parmesan cheese, half a cup
To taste, add salt and pepper when cooking.

Butter for Frying
Garnish with crispy bacon bits and sage leaves, if
desired.

Instructions

Regarding Dough:

Mix the flour, eggs, water, and salt together in a bowl. Once the dough is smooth, cover it and set aside to rest for half an hour.

Regarding Filling:

2. In a bowl, combine mashed potatoes, chopped spinach, Parmesan, ricotta, salt, and pepper.

Assembly

3. Using a round cutter, roll out the dough on a floured board and cut out circles.

Put a dollop of filling in the middle of every round. Using the dough, fold the filling over to form a half-moon. Seal by pressing the edges.

Cook the dumplings in a large saucepan of boiling salted water for 3–4 minutes, or until they float to the top.

Melt the butter in a pan and cook the boiled dumplings until they turn golden brown.

Sage leaves and crispy bacon bits are optional garnishes.

These delicious Tyrolean dumplings, known as Tiroler Schlutzkrapfen, provide a taste of classic Alpine cuisine from Seefeld.

Celebrate Seefeld's holiday enthusiasm at home with these delicious meals. These recipes bring the warmth and tastes of Seefeld's Christmas into your home, bringing a joyful mood wherever you are. Enjoy the sweetness of K
kletzenbrot, the heartiness of Tiroler Schlutzkrapfen, or a glass of Tyrolean Glühwein.

Printed in Great Britain
by Amazon

33845751R00056